WHY WE GO TO THE DOCTOR

by Rosalyn Clark

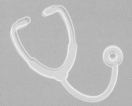

BUMBA BOOKS™

LERNER PUBLICATIONS ◆ MINNEAPOLIS

Note to Educators:

Throughout this book, you'll find critical thinking questions. These can be used to engage young readers in thinking critically about the topic and in using the text and photos to do so.

Lerner Publications Company
A division of Lerner Publishing Group, Inc.
241 First Avenue North
Minneapolis, MN 55401 USA

For reading levels and more information, look up this title at www.lernerbooks.com.

Library of Congress Cataloging-in-Publication Data

Names: Clark, Rosalyn, 1990– author.
Title: Why we go to the doctor / Rosalyn Clark.
Description: Minneapolis : Lerner Publications, [2018] | Series: Bumba books.
  Health matters | Audience: Age 4–7. | Audience: K to grade 3. | Includes
  bibliographical references and index.
Identifiers: LCCN 2017026785 (print) | LCCN 2017017242 (ebook) | ISBN
  9781512482997 (eb pdf) | ISBN 9781512482904 (lb : alk. paper) | ISBN
  9781541511095 (pb : alk. paper)
Subjects: LCSH: Physician and patient—Juvenile literature. | Communication
  in medicine—Juvenile literature.
Classification: LCC R727.3 (print) | LCC R727.3 .C525 2018 (ebook) | DDC
  610.69/6—dc23

LC record available at https://lccn.loc.gov/2017026785

Manufactured in the United States of America
1 – CG – 12/31/17

Expand learning beyond the printed book. Download free, complementary educational resources for this book from our website, www.lernerresource.com.

Table of Contents

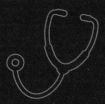

Time for a Checkup

Today we are going to the

doctor's office.

It is time for a checkup.

Doctors do important work.

They help you stay healthy.

Nurses work with doctors. Who else might work in a doctor's office?

You see the doctor when you are sick.

A doctor can give you medicine.

You see the doctor when you are hurt.

Doctors treat injuries.

What kinds of injuries might a doctor treat?

11

You also see the doctor when you feel healthy. Shots help keep you in good health.

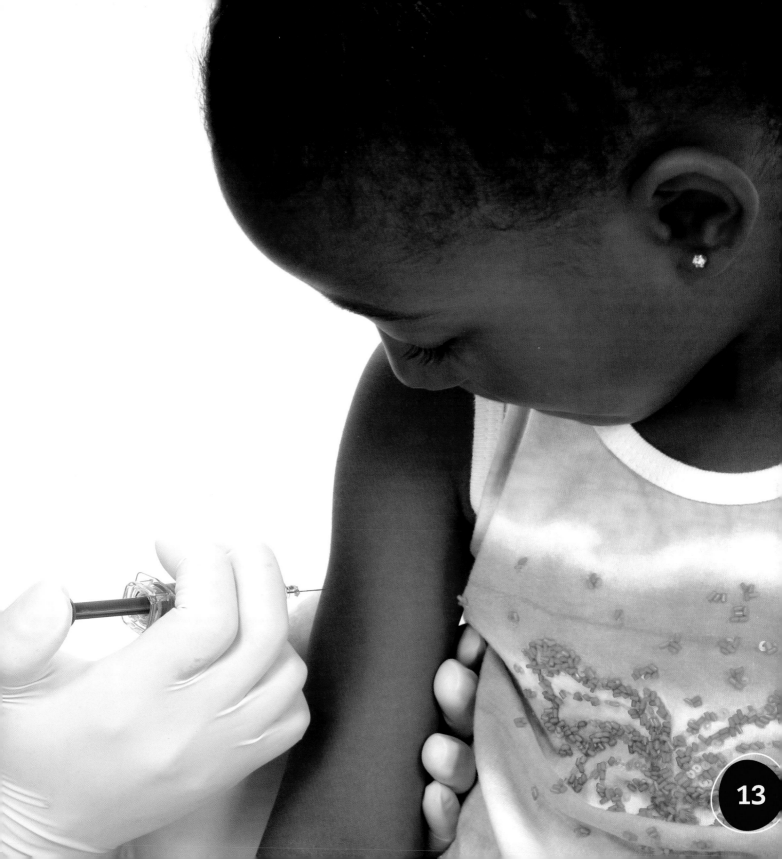

Doctors ask questions about you.

They ask if you are eating well.

They ask if you are sleeping well.

Doctors check the inside of your body.

They look into your mouth.

They look in your ears and nose.

Why do you think doctors check the inside of your body?

Doctors listen to your breathing.

They listen to your heart.

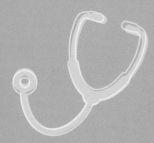

Doctors care about you.

They work hard to keep you healthy.

Things We See at the Doctor

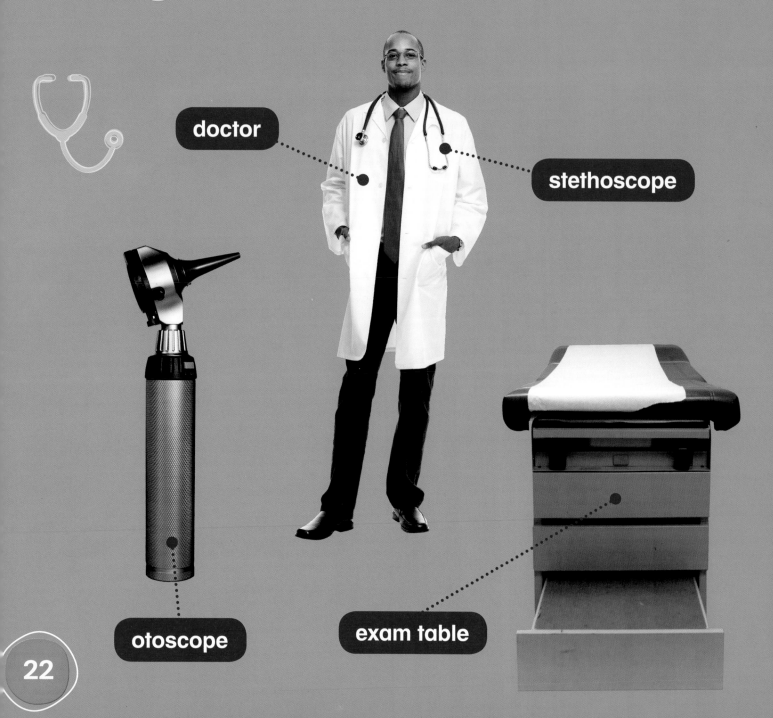

doctor

stethoscope

otoscope

exam table

Picture Glossary

checkup

an exam done by a doctor to check your health

doctor

someone who treats sick or injured people

injuries

acts that damage or hurt

medicine

something you take when you are sick

Read More

Heos, Bridget. *Let's Meet a Doctor.* Minneapolis: Millbrook Press, 2013.

Kenan, Tessa. *Hooray for Doctors!* Minneapolis: Lerner Publications, 2018.

Smith, Ian. *Going to the Doctor.* Irvine, CA: QEB Publishing, 2015.

Index

Photo Credits

The images in this book are used with the permission of: © Monkey Business Images/Shutterstock.com, pp. 5, 15, 23 (top left); © Duplass/Shutterstock.com, pp. 6–7, 12–13, 23 (bottom left); © michaeljung/iStock.com, p. 9; © alvarez/iStock.com, p. 10; © patrickheagney/iStock.com, pp. 16–17; © Dangubic/iStock.com, p. 19; © wavebreakmedia/Shutterstock.com, pp. 20, 23 (top right); © Terayut Janjaranuphab/Shutterstock.com, p. 22 (left); © kurhan/Shutterstock.com, p. 22 (middle); © bitterfly/iStock.com, p. 22 (right); © vgajic/iStock.com, p. 23 (bottom right).

Front Cover: © didesign021/Shutterstock.com.